I dedicate this book to

My Husband, Bruce,
who always believes in me.

My children, Anthony and Abby,
my two biggest fans.

My mother,
who had the patience to teach me to sew.

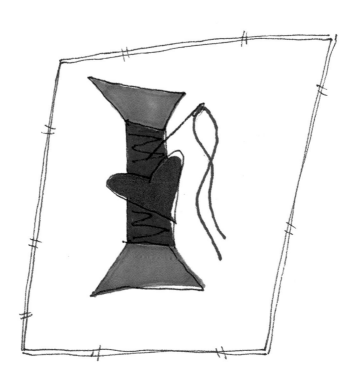

My father, whose big toe always found
the sewing pin stuck in the living room carpet.

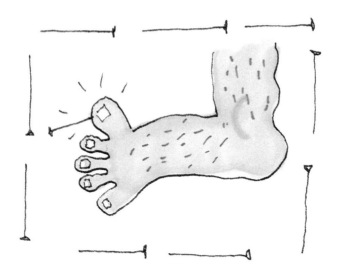

And to my two sisters,
Linda and Brenda,
who suffer from this same disease.

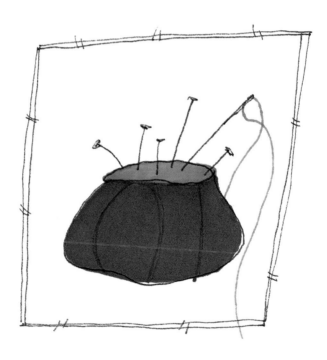

Living The Life Of a Fabric-aholic

Written and Illustrated by

Sandy Gervais

Hi, my name is Sandy

and I am a Fabric-aholic.

I once was fabric free

for five whole years.

Then one day,

as I was driving along,

I saw a sign which read,

Quilt Shop 1/2 mile.

I thought to myself,

"What could it hurt?"

I limited myself to buying

one pattern and the

four pieces of fabric that

it called for.

As I left the shop, I thought,

"Yes! I have this under control."

Well, I found out that the statement,

"once you are a fabric-aholic

you are only one yard away

from being hooked," is very true.

On my next three week binge,

I bought twenty-two yards of fabric

in one-eighth-yard increments.

I was hooked again! I was again

living the roller coaster life

of a fabric addict.

I am now out of control.

I find myself buying those six new,

red prints at the quilt shop, even though

I already have seventeen red prints at

home - only to discover

I already have two of the prints.

I find myself buying fabric that

I have no idea what I will do with it,

but I'll think of something. I must say

that piece of fabric does make a

nice place for the cat to sleep.

Yesterday I bought new fabric

to make a pattern

that I already have fabric for,

but that fabric went with

the house we lived in

three moves ago.

And now it's starting to interfere with my work. I was driving to a business meeting when I decided to stop at a quilt shop that was right on the way. I just had to go six miles north, five miles east over a one-lane bridge, and then right at the chicken farm to the first place on the left. I had no idea it would take so long to drive such a short distance!

And how was I supposed to tell

the difference between a

chicken farm and a turkey farm?

Oh well, at least I did make it to the

last fifteen minutes of the meeting.

I am now reading the help wanted

section of the newspaper.

It's probably a blessing in disguise,

because that job was at a fabric store.

My husband thought this would be great

because I would get a discount on all of

the fabric I purchased. Well, that didn't

work out so well - my first check

was a negative $226.50.

One day, when I was on one of my

all day fabric binges - it wasn't even

noon yet, and I had already been to

five different fabric shops within

a three hundred mile radius,

and had bought forty-two different

pieces of fabric. As I came up over a hill,

there was my biggest fear,

a fabric-check roadblock.

I quickly shoved my packages under the seat. The
officer, Fabric Check Freddie, walked over to the
car, as I rolled down my window. He said,
"Ma'am, we're doing a fabric check to see if you
are carrying excess fabric." I lied. "Of course
not!" I said. He said he thought he could smell
new fabric, and I quickly shoved my purse over
the hole in my car seat as I convinced him that I
had just reupholstered the car seats. My mouth
was dry, my palms were sweaty, but in a few
short minutes I was on my way to the next
fabric shop. And now I had become a liar, too.

My addiction affects the whole family. I'm so busy quilting that I never seem to get the everyday household chores done. My husband and children never have matched socks. I have been known to hide the clothes basket full of unsorted socks in the attic and buy new ones.

I forgot to feed the cat,

and when I did remember

to feed it, I inadvertantly gave it

quilt scraps instead of table scraps.

The vet's bill was $262.50.

My addiction just isn't to fabric, it's also everything related to fabric. I once saw a buttons-for-sale ad in the paper, and I called the woman and made an appointment to see the buttons.

There were fifty-two jars in all, and each jar contained some really interesting buttons. I just couldn't leave without buying all of the jars.

When I came home, my husband
asked me if I had bought the buttons.
"Yes," I said. He asked where they
were, and I said, "In the trunk."
Obviously thinking I had bought a couple
of jars, he wanted to know why I
hadn't brought them into the house.
I told him I needed help carrying them
in. That night I caught him looking up
psychiatric care in the Yellow Pages.

Every day I wake up with new hope.

I start the morning out by reading

Coping With Fabric Addiction.

By afternoon I'm reading

Quilt Top In An Hour.

A fabric sale can cause me to lose control.

There are some fabrics that I would never

consider buying - until someone puts a

ten-percent-off sign on the bolt.

Then, of course, I automatically buy

three yards because it seems like three yards

should be enough to make just about anything.

Until years later when I finally go to use that

piece of fabric and I find I am

one-half yard short!

If someone should put a one-half off sign
on the bolt, I've been known to take the
whole bolt. I don't have a clue what I
will do with it, but at that price I will
think of something. If nothing else, I can
make boxer shorts out of it, right?
Or aren't wool boxer shorts a good idea?

I once bought a bolt of mauve-colored
fabric. Why, I don't know - it must have
been half-off. I don't like the color mauve.
It looks terrible on me. In fact, I don't
know too many people who do look good in
mauve - the cat doesn't even look good
sleeping on mauve-colored fabric.

Of course, any time a shop has a sale, I develop, what my husband says, is more of an inventory problem - too much inventory. He thinks that if I would drag out all of my bags, boxes, and baskets of fabric, I would have enough yardage to open my own fabric shop. Me, owning a fabric shop, now wouldn't that be a frightening thought? Do you suppose I would ever sell any fabric, or would I just keep bringing it home for myself? If I had a sale, would I bring my fabric home in three yard pieces instead of one-eighth-yard pieces?

Quilting is a very hard concept

for my husband to understand.

He wants to know why anyone would

take pieces of fabric, cut them in

small pieces, and then sew them

back together to make a big piece.

He also doesn't understand why I need

forty-three different pieces of red fabric.

After all, isn't red, red? I told him that I

can't use the same red for everything.

I need apple red, Santa red, cherry red,

clown red, fire red, leaf red, rainbow red,

watermelon red, and many more reds

that I might have a use for sometime.

After struggling with this addiction
for several years, I felt like I truly was
starting to gain control. Then a fabric
company contacted me to design fabric
for them. I started to shake. I couldn't
believe it! What could be more fun than
designing the very thing that I was so
much in love with? I said, "Yes!"
I wound up with eighteen different
designs in five different color groups.

Of course, I would have to buy one yard of each piece. Then I was told if I bought five yards of each piece I could get it at a reduced price, and if I bought a bolt of each, I could get it for an even more reduced price. Well, let's see, I certainly will have to make myself a quilt out of my fabric. And of course, one for each of my two children, and my mother, and my two sisters. Okay, I will take ninety bolts. Why not? I will get the best savings that way. The rent on the storage shed is $250 a month.

I went to an estate auction the other day. The deceased definately suffered from the same sickness I do. There were three flat bed trailers full of boxes of old fabric, and many, many unfinished quilt tops. The lady standing next to me at the auction commented that this lady must never have finished anything and that she obviously had no control when it came to buying fabric. She obviously did not under- stand, but I could relate. I bought three boxes of fabric and six unfinished quilt tops with every intention of finishing them - someday.

On my way home from the auction,

I had a thought on what my death

notice and sale bill might read like:

WOMAN LOSES LIFE IN FREAK ACCIDENT

A local woman, Sandy Selvedge, recently lost her life in a freak home accident. She was crushed to death under a mountain of fabric when she opened a closet door. She appeared to be getting ready to make a quilt, as the book *Quilt Top In An Hour* was found nearby.

A delivery man, ironically, delivering a package of fabric, discovered the body. No one else was injured in the accident. Her cat was found nearby, shaken, but unharmed. Why any one person had so much fabric in a closet remains a mystery.

The family asks that all memorials be directed to Fabric-aholics Anonymous.

TO SETTLE THE ESTATE OF SANDY SELVEDGE THE FOLLOWING WILL BE OFFERED FOR SALE:

FOR SALE:

Many boxes of cotton print fabrics

Many boxes of wool fabrics

Many boxes of assorted fabric scraps

Several unfinished quilt tops (Six of them are <u>very</u> old)

Many <u>complete</u> <u>bolts</u> of fabric

Many jars of buttons

Many boxes of various laces and trims

Several boxes of sewing thread

Many boxes of craft patterns

Many pairs of scissors

Several boxes of tape measures

Many never been used thimbles

Several sewing machines, as is

Several boxes of craft and sewing projects in various
        stages of completion

Many, many more sewing items too numerous to list

Due to the large quantity of items to be sold, this auction will be held at the World Trade Center, over a three-day period. Food and lodging will be available.

AUCTIONEER'S NOTE: We have never seen such a large amount of fabric and sewing-related items. Come plenty early to view all the items.

I hope someday I can kick this

addiction, but for now, I'm just

taking it one yard at a time.

The End.

About the author

Sandy Gervais has been sewing since she was seven years old. She made her first sewing project while staying at her grandparents' house. Her grammie, as she called her grandmother, gave her an old white sheet and told her she could make doll clothes out of it. Instead she made a jacket and skirt for playing dress-up. The entire outfit was sewn by hand as grammie was afraid she would sew her fingers with the machine. Sandy did not quite have "allow for movement" down to a science. She had to take tiny, tiny steps when she wore that suit.

Soon after that she made a turquoise, gathered skirt and a simple blouse for her first 4-H project. Her mother then taught her things about ease to allow for movement, clipping curves, and trimming seams. And this time she used the sewing machine. Sandy has been sewing and "collecting" fabric ever since.

Sandy is a self-taught artist. She combines her art and her sewing ability to create folk art wall quilts. These quilts are then adapted into patterns so people can make them for their own enjoyment.

Sandy is known for using unusual embellishments on her wall quilts such as tin, twigs, wire, and antique buttons.

Sandy resides in Algona, Iowa, with her husband, Bruce, and her two children, Anthony and Abby.

For a colored catalog of Sandy's patterns, contact:

Pieces From My Heart
P.O. Box 112
Algona, IA 50511
(515)295-5672